Embracing Success
Through Customer Service

Embracing Success
Through Customer Service

By
Joy Kelshall

Copyright © Joy Kelshall 2012

All rights reserved. No part of this publication may be reproduced or transmitted in any form or by any means, electronic or mechanical, including photocopy, recording, any information storage or retrieval system, or on the internet, without permission in writing from the publishers.

ISBN: 978-976-8244-03-1

Published by Joy Kelshall

E-mail: joykelshall@gmail.com

By the same Author:
Embracing Success Through Time Management
ISBN 978-976-8054-91-3

Embracing Success Through Customer Service (Hard Cover)
ISBN 978-976-8054-78-4

Design & Layout by Paria Publishing Company Limited
Printed by Lightning Source
Second Edition 2012

Flamboyant painting: © Lisa O'connor

Contents

Preface	VI
Dedication	VII
Appreciation	VIII
Introduction	XI

Chapter 1	I adopted Customer Service as a Principle	1
Chapter 2	Adopting Customer Service as a Principle	7
Chapter 3	The Customer	15
Chapter 4	Customers' Expectations	25
Chapter 5	Customer Service	31
Chapter 6	Quality of Service versus Price	35
Chapter 7	Profitability	39
Chapter 8	Customer Service Skills	43
Chapter 9	Dress and Grooming	47
Chapter 10	Appropriate Behavior at Work	62
Chapter 11	Business Manners	66
Chapter 12	Delivering Quality Customer Care at the Workplace in a Nutshell	83
Chapter 13	Communication	88
Chapter 14	Skills for Challenging Customers	102
Chapter 15	Benefits	107
Conclusion		110

Dedication

For Lee and Jamie, who taught me the delight that providing excellent service brings.

Preface

I am greatly honored to be asked to write this preface as an ordinary person owning and operating a small professional business, which requires constant vigilance in all aspects of the business for it to prosper.

In constantly seeking ways to improve, we all seek advice on what can be done and it did not take me long to realize that good customer service is a major component of success in both a personal and business sense.

Reading this book has proved invaluable as a guide and companion in the effort to develop and improve good customer service.

It is one important area in which a small input results in major benefits, and this clear, unambiguous book is of enormous help in achieving the goal of good customer service.

As the old saying goes, "Nothing succeeds like success".

Mr. Lee Kelshall
(Attorney at Law
& Notary Public)

Appreciation

When I decided to write this book my intention was not to introduce new ideas about how to provide great service. That has already long been done – many times over. I wanted to find the best way possible – working with the same, aged-old concept of excellent service – to persuade you to grasp the true essence of how adopting customer service as a principle will guarantee that you always deliver exceptional service and thereby embrace success.

I could not have done it without the support of my family and friends. I am particularly grateful to Gwenneth Moore, Larry Agge and Cathryn Kelshall for their input, *"words of wisdom"* and encouragement.

Special thanks to my producer, Dominic Besson, for his patience and guidance in the design and layout of *"Embracing Success…"*

Then there is my favorite artist, Lisa O'Connor, who painted the beautiful flamboyant tree which graces many pages of this book. Thank you, Lisa; you added that special touch of beauty that you alone know how to do.

I also feel extremely blessed to have worked for a wonderful airline, which provided me with many of the *"excellent service"* opportunities I shared with you in this book.

Finally and always there is my amazing husband, Lee, and our gem of a daughter, Jamie, who were not only my greatest critiques but my rock and my best friends ever! Thank you Lee and Jamie, without you both, I could not have done it.

I feel about my book how Mark Twain felt, when he said;

*"My books are water;
those of the great geniuses are wine...
everybody drinks water."*

Happy reading!

Joy Kelshall

XII

Introduction

"Books are the quietest and most constant of friends; they are the most accessible and wisest of counselors and the most patient of teachers." (Charles W. Elliot)

There are numerous books, DVDs, training programs and other diverse sources available to enlighten one about excellent customer service. Their messages are alike in that they all echo ways to better manage customers. This book also has a similar message but its echo offers an additional, interesting concept of *adopting customer service as a principle*. What is a principle? Simply put it is *"a truth or belief that is accepted as a base for reasoning or action."* Many of these resources have recorded information which upholds the principle of customer service, however I want to go a step further and encourage you to not just accept and uphold the principle of customer service, but more importantly, I want you to adopt customer service as a principle.

Think about the word, *"adopt"* and reflect on the images this conjures up in your imagination. What do you see? The Oxford dictionary defines *"adopt"* as to *"choose an option or course of action"* or *"take on an attitude or position"*. If you were to relate this definition to adopting customer service as a principle, then this would mean that you would have decided how you will be dealing with customers long before you actually come into contact with them. You would have determined your mind-set and attitude for each and every one of your impending transactions. Any dealings you have with your customers will cause you to behave in a manner which would clearly exhibit your choice of adoption.

I am sure that in your reflection you also envisaged images of adopting a child, just like I did. Most people will automatically link adoption to children. But think about it; when you adopt a child you legally take on the responsibility of accepting this child to bring up as your own. This is a decision of great magnitude to consider and much deliberation and careful planning would have taken place before you made up your mind.

It is the same with this customer service adoption theory; the preliminary significant groundwork must be done. In this book I have specified some of these prerequisites including how to dress and behave appropriately at work. In addition, the honing of your communication and listening skills and the improvement of your management of challenging customers' skills will help to strengthen your ability.

To get you more involved also with the overall content of this book, its design solicits your opinions on various relevant topics. I believe that personal participation will formulate the means for you to "buy in", better understand, and appreciate it. I have also drawn from some of my personal experiences to emphasize this notion of adoption in an effort to convince you, too, to take ownership of how adopting customer service as a principle will help you to embrace success.

I worked for many years in the field of aviation. After I retired, I joined a training and recruitment company as a training associate. My reason for doing so was because I wanted to continue my efforts to share with as many people as possible the importance of excellent customer service. This is also why I chose to write this book. I know that a better understanding of adopting customer service as a principle will change the lens through which we see customers and treat with them. The Rev. Dr. Martin Luther King Jr. once said, *"Cowardice asks the question; Is it safe? Expediency asks the question; Is it politic? Vanity asks the question; Is it popular? But conscience asks the question; Is it right? And there comes a time when one must take a position that is neither safe politic, nor popular. But he takes it because his conscience tells him it is right."* I believe adopting customer service as a principle (*"a truth or belief that is accepted as a base for reasoning and action; a moral rule or set of ideas which guides behavior"*) is the right position to take.

After reading this book, you will be able to:

- *Adopt customer service as a principle and define exactly what that means.*
- *Determine who your customers are and better understand their expectations.*
- *Describe customer service and acknowledge the impact that it has on an organization's profitability.*
- *Better understand the importance of how to dress and behave at work.*
- *Communicate with customers using active listening techniques and develop more confidence.*
- *Identify skills for dealing with challenging customers*
- *List benefits from providing positive customer service experiences*
- *Build long-lasting relationships with customers.*

Chapter 1
I adopted Customer Service as a Principle

"As the water shapes itself to the vessel that contains it, so a wise man adapts himself to circumstances." (Confucius)

*I*magine for a moment that I am holding a glass filled with some water and I ask, *"Is this glass of water half-full or half-empty?"* Answers to that familiar question I am sure, will vary since some people will see a half-full glass, some will view a half-empty one, and others will merely notice a glass with some water in it. The different answers to this age-old, rhetorical question have generally been interpreted to explain one's attitude to life. That is, if you see a half full glass, you are considered to be an optimist whose focus is on the good things in life. You have a positive attitude and believe that things will always improve. Symbolically you see the glass already half full and continuing to be filled right up to the top. If, however, you see a half empty glass, this implies that you are a pessimist whose concentration is on what is lacking in your life. Your attitude is a negative one with no hope for relief. Metaphorically you believe the water in the glass will continue to deplete until there is nothing left. Of course if you merely observe a glass with some water in it you may just be saying, *"The glass is just twice as big as it needs to be."*! 😊

Be that as it may, it never ceases to amaze me how we can each look at exactly the same thing, but interpret it differently. I have introduced this common expression simply because I want to convince us all to *"see"* and interpret customer service in only one way possible - as a principle (*"a set of ideas which guides behavior"*) and so be persuaded to adopt it. This concept will help to reinforce the message of what excellent service is. Some of the relevant skills needed to consistently deliver exceptional service are also highlighted because, in addition to adopting this theory, it is equally important to implement or *"grow"* it. As Goethe said, *"Knowing is not enough, we must apply. Willing is not enough, we must do."*

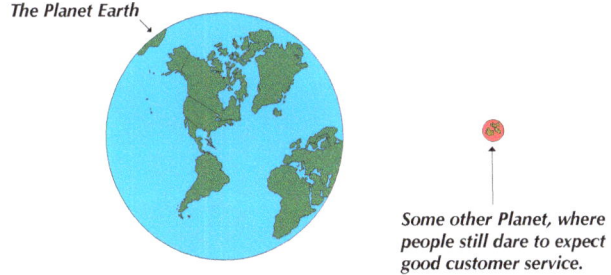

The Planet Earth

Some other Planet, where people still dare to expect good customer service.

Having spent over twenty-five years in the In-flight department of the aviation industry, I have interacted with people from all different walks of life. I discovered that it was easy to *"see, a "half-full glass"* while delivering service when things were running smoothly. However, when faced with delays, disgruntled passengers, over-weight bags, and other difficult situations, the job became progressively more challenging, and the glass seemed much emptier. What is the secret then, to be able to consistently and graciously deliver excellent customer service, despite the circumstances? It took a harrowing experience for me to figure it out.

One day I was on a flight heading for home. The aircraft was on taxi for take-off from one of our beautiful Caribbean islands. It was a glorious day and we, the cabin crew, were exhausted but happy because the next landing was home and our last stop for the day. Suddenly, over the intercom we heard *"Purser to cockpit"*. Immediately my heart stopped beating and I literally froze for exactly two seconds, while waiting for further instructions. *"Purser to cockpit"* was an emergency signal from the cockpit to the cabin and we knew our captain was telling us that something was terribly wrong. It turned out that one of our engines was on fire and we were in reality faced with a life and death situation.

Instinctively, when the instruction came, our training *"kicked in"* and thankfully, as trained, we automatically safely evacuated the passengers. That experience taught me a lesson in service I will never forget. In a worst case scenario as a cabin crew member, I was not only expected to do what I was trained to do and safely evacuate the passengers but I was also expected to comfort and calm them for some time after the ordeal. I had to cloak my own personal, traumatized feelings. That took some gumption that even I did not know I had!

After that incident however, the importance of being competently trained to do my job will be forever stamped on my brain. I knew, though, that as important as it was something more was needed to enable me to cope with unexpected or difficult situations. I believe on that eventful day, it didn't matter what the circumstances were, or even in how many different ways I may have chosen to deal with them, in the end as terrified as our passengers were, they knew and were satisfied that I had not only done my job but also that all of the crew had given it our best shot. Therefore, customer satisfaction does not always depend on the customer getting what is wanted, (which in this instance, was getting to Trinidad on time) but rather on how we managed the unexpected situation, for the best result.

I carefully pondered this and after dwelling long and hard on the *"what ifs?"* I came to the conclusion that when providing any service, expected or unexpected, the dealings should always be a positive one. How can one do this? What can one focus on to make all relations positive? I believe the only possible answer lies in this fact - one's mindset and attitude should be programmed to react in a particular manner whenever the occasion demands. In the exact same way, as cabin crew, we involuntarily responded to the command to evacuate passengers. This could only occur if one adopted the concept that customer service is a principle. Then that could become the inspiration and guiding light for how to always best serve customers. This means therefore that if we were to replace the water in the glass with service, and collectively all *"see"*, interpret, and adopt this service as a principle, we will always only see *"a half-full glass,"* and our customers will be satisfied with their experiences.

Chapter 2
Adopting Customer Service as a Principle

"To know what is right and not do it is the worst cowardice" (Confucius)

"Hey! That was my stop back there."

We have defined a principle as *"a truth or belief that is accepted as a base for reasoning and action"* and *"a moral rule or set of ideas which guides behavior."* I truly believe that choosing to adopt customer service as a principle is a life-long commitment to service excellence. To better understand this theory, let us identify some other principles.

What are some principles that people generally accept?

_____
_____
_____
_____
_____
_____

You may have identified these:

These principles and many others are all bounded by specific parameters of how one should behave to demonstrate them. For example, in an office scenario it may be said *"It's not that I object to Kevin using the phone, it's the principle of the thing."* The principle being, that it is an office phone and Kevin should be mindful of this and not take time off to make personal calls at the company's expense. This and many other examples are decided by accepted beliefs that rule the world, no matter where you live or with whom you work. It relates to ethics, - ethics being a system of moral behavior.

Let us now closely examine the principle of service. Service in *"customer service"* refers to the attention/help you will give to your customers. A principle according to the dictionary is *"a truth or belief that is accepted as a base for reasoning and action"* or *"a moral rule or set of ideas which guides behavior"*. This clearly establishes that our behavior therefore when serving others will be influenced by what is the accepted right or wrong way to do so. If we choose the right behavior we will be demonstrating good service. If we choose the wrong one then obviously we will provide bad service. If you want to automatically respond favorably to customers then your mindset, attitude and actions should be programmed to behave in what is the accepted and correct response. Adopting customer service as a principle is the key to this automated response. It becomes a habit (*"a preference or tendency"*) which gets harder to break the more you practise it. *"We are what we repeatedly do. Excellence then, is not an act, but a habit."* (Aristotle)

In addition you can support this attitude by choosing behavior which upholds other truths like respect and honesty. Imagine trying to give good service without respect and honesty. It just won't work since these principles operate hand in hand to make excellent customer service a *"way of life."* It was Charles R. Swindoll who said, *"Words can never adequately convey the incredible impact of our attitude toward life. The longer I live the more I become convinced that life is ten percent what happens to us and ninety percent how we respond to it"*.

Mind you, despite our mind-set it is not always easy to practice these home truths. It can be difficult to work with customers who display blatant disregard for these ethics. For instance, as crew members in the airline, our operations were guided by a chain of command which we all respected. The Captain was ultimately in-charge of a flight but we, the cabin crew, were directly supervised by a purser. On some flights, (I must mention – very few of them) we would get a purser whose ethics were questionable. It was very tempting then to bypass her and go directly to the Captain if we were faced with a demanding situation. But even though at those times it may have been very difficult to work with her, we always showed respect for her status and did not by-pass her. This enabled us to deal with the matter at hand in a professional manner. By concentrating on the issue and not the personality, we were able to work harmoniously.

At the end of the day remember it is not what you do, but *"also what we do not do, for which we are accountable"* (Moliere). To ensure that your accountability can pass the tests you have to always choose the right behavior. You can do this if you build an infrastructure to support your beliefs. You can do this firstly, by consciously opting to adopt customer service as a principle and secondly, by following up and learning how to cement these beliefs. This preparation will include gaining the relevant knowledge and then putting it into practice. It explains to you the proper way to dress and behave at work. It will also allow you to improve your listening and communication skills and helps you to deal professionally with even challenging customers.

A bonus which you will get from this adoption theory is that you are inspired to have the discipline to maintain a healthy life style. This makes it so much easier to deal with not only routine incidents but also the challenging ones. After all if you have had a good night's sleep it will allow you to be better able to *"face the world"*.

Serving people in the best way possible is not as easy as it seems. It requires a conscious choice of behavior since as humans we are susceptible to our own concerns. We have our own problems and *"baggage"* making it not always easy to be nice to others. This can occasionally cause our emotions to compete with our choice of behavior. However if we adopt customer service as a principle it will become a habit for us to unconsciously make the right choice and always act appropriately.

This decision will allow you to go the extra mile. I recall the time I got my brand new car. I remember how my elation took a steep downturn as my beautiful new car randomly started stalling on me. The worst part was whenever the mechanics examined it, she purred and they could not identify any problems. After eight months of this torture, the managing director of the automobile company decided to keep the car overnight and use it to drive himself home. Lo and behold!! It stalled on him on the highway and he had to call his mechanics to rescue him. The next day he instructed his staff to locate the source of this problem and fix it. The best part though was when he handed me keys to a brand new car and apologized profusely about the anxiety he imagined I must have faced. I did not expect to get a brand new vehicle. I assumed that they would fix the other one for me. However by choosing to go the extra mile and replace my car, I, to this day, remain a loyal customer with that company.

I can also recall many times that I have received great service. Like the time the bakery forgot to bake the cake we had ordered for our three years old daughter's birthday party. They not only apologized and accepted responsibility for the mix-up, but they promised to deliver a cake to our home in time for the party. I must say I had my reservations about this promise and was already disappointed because the cake I had ordered was not now available. Imagine my surprise when they went the extra mile and actually delivered the cake, which was supposed to be unavailable, before her party began. This was the Sesame Street birthday cake which was what our daughter really wanted. Now that was fantastic service!!

I am sure you too can think of different times when others went the extra mile to provide you with great service. Take some time and write down at least one occasion someone went beyond the call of duty for you.

_____
_____
_____
_____

_____
_____
_____
_____
_____
_____
_____
_____
_____
_____
_____

Going the extra mile helps to build strong loyal relationships and is a sure way to retain customers. A part of the vision statement of the airline I worked for referred to *"the warmth of the Caribbean"*. I believe that using principles as our guide, helps to make it easier to nurture the *"warmth"* of human relationships to guarantee our customers' satisfaction

Chapter 3

The Customer

"The superior man is slow in his words and earnest in his conduct." (Confucius)

Whether it is going to the grocery, shopping for new clothes, jet-setting to New York or filling up with petrol at the gas station, we interact with many people during the course of a day. These interactions could create mystical magical moments or monotonous and miserable ones. A smile, a *"good morning"*, a welcome greeting, a *"How may I help you?"* as opposed to a snub, a growl or an unapproachable manner are all tangibles which set the stage for these interactions. As we continue on this journey to further explore the concept of adopting customer service as a principle, let us first consider how we would like to be treated as a customer. As a customer how would you prefer to be treated?

Using the letters which spell, "customer service", write a word or phrase to relate how you would like to be treated as a customer.

CUSTOMER

C-
U-
S-
T-
O-
M-
E-
R-

SERVICE

S-
E-
R-
V-
I -
C-
E-

Possible answers you may have written are:

CUSTOMER

C- courteous; caring; creative
U- understanding; unique
S- smile; supportive; serve
T- truthful; teamwork; tactful
O- open-minded; opportunity
M- meet expectations; motivate
E- empathy; essential; extra
R- range; ready; reasonable

SERVICE

S- sensitive; sincere; satisfy
E- enthusiastic; encouraging; engaging
R- respectful; results; remember
V- value; versatile; validate
I- integrity; involved; interested
C- communicate; contact
E- effectively; efficiently; excellent

Now that you have ascertained how you would like to be treated as a customer, let us recognize who are customers. Identifying who customers are will help you to focus on how they too may prefer to be treated. If you were to ask them how they would like to be dealt with I am absolutely certain that their answers will be very similar to that of yours. What is amazing is that both your responses will include some of the guiding principles mentioned in the previous chapter. Principles which work hand in hand with the principle of customer service. This highlights the significance of adopting customer service as a principle since you will want to *"do unto others as you would have them do unto you"*.

Make a list of who are your internal and external customers and also write a definition for a *"customer"*.

Internal customers	External customers

A customer is _____

Three other definitions for a *"customer"* are:

- *"A customer is anyone who ultimately benefits from the service/products he is offered or benefits from a relationship with an organization."*

- *"A customer is the most important visitor on our premises. He is not dependant on us, we are dependant on him. He is not an interruption in our work, he is the purpose of it. He is not an outsider in our business, he is a part of it. We are not doing him a favor by serving him, he is doing us a favor by giving us an opportunity to do so." (Mahatma Gandhi)*

- *The consumer – that is the ultimate user of a product or a service – is always a customer." Peter Drucker*

External customers you may have identified will be anyone who requires your product or service. They represent the many publics we deal with on an everyday basis. During my career as a cabin crew member, most of the people who boarded the aircraft were called *"passengers"*. Even though we thought it best to refer to them as our *"guests"*, they represented the bulk of our external customers. The external customer is the main reason why a company does business. This is because he is the one who buys its products or services and this sale is what the success of the business relies on.

Some of the internal customers you may have identified would be your colleagues, staff members, suppliers, buyers, managers and even include the cleaning crew at the office. It is easy to disregard these internal people as your customers. However the expression, *"Charity begins at home"* may be a useful one to embrace here since your internal customers are valuable assets. They have feelings and emotions just like you and I and require the nurturing and care just like the external ones. It is always more difficult to deal with them than with machines since you can't press *"delete"* or a switch to turn them off.

A sure way to achieve excellent internal customer relations is to base them on the principles of respect, regard, caring and competence. Each of us has a responsibility to practice excellent internal customer care despite our status in the company. Much of this can be accomplished if it is founded on the principle of trust. Trust will be difficult to gain in an organization when management treats its employees with a lack of respect and vice versa. It is said, that trust *"takes years to build and a few seconds to destroy"*. How we handle ourselves on an on-going, day to day basis can improve our internal relations and result in, not only harmonious, sincere relationships with our colleagues, but ultimately in loyalty, profit and goodwill for the organization. It is always important to learn *"how"* to handle what life actually gives us.

22 Chapter 3: The Customer

We can change our troubles into treasures, and I found this interesting poem which says it all.

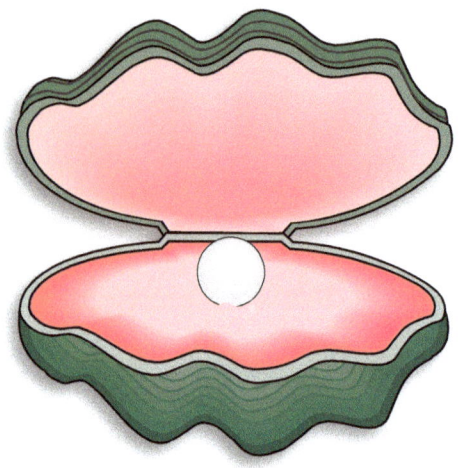

There once was an oyster
Whose story I'll tell,
Who found that some sand
Had worked under his shell.
Just one little grain
But it gave him some pain
(For oysters have feelings
That are very plain)
Now did he berate
This working of fate,
That left him in such a
Deplorable state?
Did he curse the government?

Call for an election?
Or gripe that the sea
Should have given protection?
No! He said to himself
As he sat on the shelf,
"Since I cannot remove it,
I think I'll improve it."
Well, years passed by,
As years usually do,
Till he came to his destiny,
Oyster stew!!
But the small grain of sand
That had bothered him so,
Was a beautiful pearl
All richly aglow.
Now this tale has a moral,
For isn't it grand,
What an oyster can do
With a small grain of sand?
And what couldn't we do
If we'd only begin
With all of the things
That get under our skin?
(Author Unknown)

The simple thought of *"I cannot remove it so let me improve it"* can be life-changing. We can all learn from the oyster when dealing with both our internal and external customers.

Successful companies have, and continue to maintain, healthy relationships with both internal and external customers. The Ritz-Carlton, a chain of hotels renowned for their outstanding service, says that its success is based on a simple philosophy; *"To take care of customers, you must first take care of those who take care of customers."* It stands to reason that satisfied staff will deliver high service value, which in turn will create satisfied customers. Satisfied customers in turn will produce more sales and profits for the organization. This is really what it is all about and everybody wins. We are obliged to have good internal customer relations to be successful with our external ones. We must therefore consistently strive to correct, maintain and enhance our customer service experiences with both our internal and external customers. Using the principles of trust, respect and loyalty, to name a few, will help us to meet our obligation of being successful with all our customers.

Chapter 4

Customers' Expectations

"Forewarned, forearmed; to be prepared is half the victory." (Spanish proverb)

We now know who most of our customers are and we are aware of how they would like to be treated. Discerning their expectations is the next step in our quest for customer service excellence. Bear in mind that these expectations will vary with each customer. Having adopted customer service as a principle the goal now is to not only meet but to surpass these expectations. As a cabin crew member I can attest that our passengers/guests expected us to be the chief-cook and bottle-washer, and more!! For example, mothers with babies expected us to help them look after the young ones on a flight.

Business executives whose needs were totally different, also expected first class service, changing us from baby sitters to executive assistants in seconds!

List what you believe your customers expect.

Customers' Expectations:

_____
_____
_____
_____
_____
_____
_____
_____
_____
_____
_____
_____

Customers when dealing with organizations generally expect;

- *Quality service - this begins with a warm, polite greeting which sets the tone for the interaction. "You only have one chance to make a first impression" is an aged, old expression that could be adopted as your mantra.*
- *Reliability*
- *Respect*
- *Competitive prices*
- *Comfortable, attractive, safe and accessible locations*
- *Discounts*
- *Trained, well groomed, polite, and knowledgeable staff with good communication skills.*
- *Prompt service*
- *User-friendly processes*
- *After sales service*
- *Value for their money*

Those very same principles which guide our behavior will once again be in demand if we are to meet and surpass our customers' expectations. If we adopt customer service as a principle we will incorporate these and surpassing our customers' expectations will be a *"piece of cake"*.

Interestingly enough on the other side of the coin would be the things that customers do not expect and even actually dislike. I have listed some of them below and I think it would be a good idea for you to personally decide which one of them rings true. If you choose more than one of them, that's okay too. Underline the one(s) you really do not appreciate.

Do you never expect or even dislike it when someone who is serving you:

1. *Chews gum*
2. *Speaks very loudly*
3. *Never makes eye contact*
4. *Carries on another conversation either on the phone or with a colleague*
5. *Displays negative body language like slouching or sprawling back on his chair*
6. *Makes you feel like you are imposing on his time*
7. *Is rude and impatient*
8. *Speaks down to you*
9. *Sings or dances to background music*
10. *Follows you around when you really need some space to look around*

Continue the list if you have others:

Chapter 5

Customer Service

"Skill and confidence are an unconquered army." (George Herbert)

We can now recognize who our customers are and we also have the recipe to surpass their expectations. Taking time out to now define exactly what customer service is will help us discover the *"how"* in delivering outstanding service. Write a short definition for what you think customer service is.

Customer service is:

_____
_____
_____
_____
_____
_____

Other definitions are:

- *Customer service is a principle.*
- *"Customer service is anything we do for the customer which enhances his experience."*
- *"Any contact whether active or passive between a customer and a company that causes a positive perception by the customer."*
- *"Doing ordinary things, extraordinary."*
- *"Taking care of customers as you would like to be treated."*
- *"Adding value and integrity to every customer interaction."*
- *"Whatever your customer thinks it is."*

The above definitions regard customer service as having a positive influence on the customer. Customer service is seen as a benefit or plus for the customer and that is exactly how we want to consistently regard it. Does that mean the customer always gets what he wants and that he is always right? Absolutely not!! It does mean though that after the contact between you and the customer is over, he leaves satisfied with how you handled the situation.

Situations differ and they frequently require you to use different approaches. However, whatever you do must leave the customer satisfied with how you did it. This can be trying at times, especially when you are dealing with a customer who you know will not be buying your product or service. There are times when you will feel that you are wasting your time and energy. If however you have adopted customer service as a principle, at these times, you will automatically react in a proper manner displaying courtesy and respect. You may not get a sale but you will create goodwill which is very difficult to put a value on. Think of how many other customers this customer will tell of your interaction. Chances are you will get much more than a single sale in the future because of it. Lack of goodwill jeopardizes the reputation and image of your company. Customers definitely cannot be ignored or mishandled when providing service, even if they are not buying or even if you cannot provide exactly what they want.

I recall an incident on a London flight when a passenger insisted on an upgrade from economy class to first class because the flight was two hours delayed. This however was not a decision I could make, especially since the delay was due to inclement weather and totally beyond the control of the airline. I empathized with his dilemma, explained my position and offered instead to change his seat to a more comfortable one at the bulkhead, which provided much more leg room. He was thrilled, appreciated my attempt to assist and agreed to accept my offer. It worked favorably for both of us, in that he did not exactly get what he wanted, but he did get a better seat. I, on the other hand, felt good, since it not only made him happier but it also made my job so much easier, having to deal with a satisfied customer.

This is why it is essential to always regard and adopt customer service as a principle. This adoption will direct you to always be searching for alternative solutions. Solutions which will enable you to do *"ordinary things, extraordinary"* and at the same time *"add value to every customer interaction"*.

Chapter 6

Quality of Service versus Price

"Action is eloquence." (Shakespeare)

Companies all over the world aggressively compete to sell their products and/or services. The competition is fierce since many of them now offer quality products at comparable prices. The customer has a variety of choices and can shop around to compare both price and quality. Before he decides to buy he may even opt to bargain with a company to get a better deal since he wants to ensure he gets value for his hard-earned cash. He is, after all, only interested in satisfying his wants and needs.

The choice he makes will usually be influenced and determined by three factors. These are namely:

- *What his perceptions are*
- *What his experiences were and*
- *What his expectations are*

He may already have preconceived ideas about what to expect when he interacts with you, based on his perceptions and/or past experiences. This is where service usually becomes the deciding factor and is, by far, more important than price. As the service provider it is important to know and fully understand these factors, so that you do not perceive, expect and assume that any customer, challenging or otherwise, is going to be difficult to manage. How you serve the customer will clinch the deal or not. Price is not the deciding factor.

During my years as a cabin attendant, I consistently had to remind myself of all these factors. I imagined that traveling could be very nerve-racking for some passengers, especially when they arrived at my domain, having finally boarded the aircraft. Think about it;

- *the packing*
- *the trip to the airport*
- *the long lines to check-in*
- *the immigration and security check points and*
- *the wait to board the aircraft*

These can add up to a long, painful and tedious experience – called stress! How each passenger dealt with these issues varied from indifference to obsession. To be better able to welcome them, put them at ease and cultivate my relationship with them, despite this *"stress"* I dared not assume, perceive or expect any of them to be any other than my *"guest"*.

The relationship between a customer and a company, after all, is a delicate one and as such must be carefully nurtured and developed for mutual benefit and repeat business. Bernie Marcus, one of the founders of Home Depot (which is a large retail home improvement chain in the United States of America) said, *"Customer cultivation is just like cultivating a tomato plant. Prepare the soil, maybe put some additives in it. Plant the seed. Prune it. Fertilize it. Apply insecticide. It will always grow bigger if you cultivate it. If you cultivate it, it will bear more fruit."*

What really matters then is that each customer is dealt with on an individual basis and that each interaction is managed in a professional and courteous manner. Behaving courteously, respectfully and professionally display the choice you made when you adopt customer service as a principle. It is this quality of service which makes the customers decide to use you as their preferred choice. Tom Peters and Nancy Austin in their book, A Passion for Excellence, wrote, *"Quality of service is more important than price. Price will bring shoppers but not customers,…. give the customer something worthwhile and she or he will pay what it's worth"*.

Chapter 7

Profitability

"Paying attention to simple little things that most men neglect makes a few men rich." (Henry Ford Sr.)

The Money Tree/Profit

Prompt service Reliability Respect Value for money After sales service

Contented and loyal customers have a huge impact on the profitability of any organization. An organization will lose customers, potential customers, sales and even goodwill which are all valuable assets, if service is compromised. Satisfied customers not only buy more but buy more often. This decision to buy more will result in increased profit for organizations. Organizations will do well to remember that *"what the customer buys and considers value is never just a product. It is always a utility, that is, what a product or service does for him"* (Peter Drucker). Companies need customers to keep on buying to create the profit which is essential for the sustainability of their businesses.

Results from customer service research state:

- *"It costs on an average, five times more in energy, resources and money to get a new customer as it is to keep an old one."*
- *"When we receive good service we will tell 9 – 12 people on average. However when we receive poor service we tell up to 20 people. (Twice the amount)"*
- *"What is the chance by percentage that customers will repurchase from a company if their complaint is handled quickly and pleasantly? Answer: 82%"*
- *"If customers received poor service, 91% of them would not come back."*
- *"A completely satisfied customer is 6 times more likely to come back."*
- *"A 5% increase in customer satisfaction will result in 25% - 85% increase in net profit."*
- *"It was discovered that 68% of customers stopped being customers because of poor service. The other 32% do so for a variety of reasons including death, moving and preferring other products and prices."*

It is important to note here that this 68% can be reduced significantly by good customer service practices.

For companies to blossom and grow it is therefore absolutely imperative that they embrace and practice the concept that customer service is a principle. Only then will they to be able to provide superior service which results in profits. Arthur Sheldon said it most appropriately, when he said, *"He profits most, who serves the best."* Quality customer care is an opportunity that no company can afford to ignore. It is frequently the distinguishing factor which differentiates one company from the other. Amazing isn't it? **One of the cheapest ways to get more profit is to simply adopt good customer service practices.**

It is very important to remember that **customer service training** is an area companies can always revisit as one in which profits can also be most easily generated. For example, many people would choose the airline I worked for, instead of the competition, because they preferred the on-board customer service they experienced with us. This was because the airline invested time and money to do regular refresher customer service training for us. This training was successful in reinforcing good service practices and reenergizing us to go back to the workplace refocused with more commitment and dedication. In return our passengers were loyal and used us as their preferred choice of air travel again and again.

It is just not good enough to initially train your staff, you must **repeatedly** retrain them to ensure this renewal of commitment and dedication. You will guarantee a high return on your training investment if you do this.

Chapter 8

Customer Service Skills

"To be a giant and not a dwarf in your profession you must always be growing."
(William Matthew)

𝒦nowing who our customers are, understanding their expectations, and adopting good service as a principle, should now be easy to grasp. Delivering quality customer care however will not happen automatically because of this. We have to learn and develop certain skills to be able to present an attractive image and successfully deal with all customers, even the challenging ones. These skills include learning:

- *How to dress and behave appropriately at work*
- *Effective communication skills*
- *Listening skills*
- *Specific skills to deal with challenging customers*

If you ran a company customers would make assumptions based on your company's outward appearance. They prefer clean, painted, attractive offices, with proper signage and a comfortable room temperature. They want, in addition, safe parking and washroom facilities. Even if your location is not as convenient as your competitor they will still choose you if you make up for this with the amenities you offer as part of your service.

In the same token they also make assumptions based on your individual appearance. They prefer neat, attractive, confident, helpful and knowledgeable staff. For example:

- *Are you easily identifiable?*
- *Are you neat, well groomed and properly dressed?*
- *Are you aware of what your image and your body language are shouting?*
- *Do you know how to behave appropriately at work?*

As a cabin crew member I was provided with a uniform. This was mainly to be easily recognized by passengers including in the event of an emergency. Even so, specific uniform and grooming regulations were strictly enforced by the airline, to ensure compliance by all crew members to maintain a good professional image. The airline recognized the important role that image played in the grand scheme of business. To further develop this image we devoted days of training on dress, grooming and social skills to new cabin crew, because we wanted them to feel confident about delivering exceptional customer service. Certainly anyone can learn how to change and improve his image to project exactly what he needs it to be.

Customers automatically judge your business by its appearance and you by yours. If you and your company adopt customer service as a principle you will naturally be prepared to present yourselves in the most suitable facades to project the right images.

Chapter 9

Dress and Grooming

"I am sure that nothing has such a decisive influence upon a man's course as his personal appearance, and not so much his appearance, as his belief in its attractiveness or unattractiveness."
(Leo Tolstoy)

Dress and grooming have a remarkable influence on your service skills. If you feel good about your appearance the chances are that your actions will reflect this. People also usually expect your behavior to match how you are dressed. How you dress for work must show respect for your profession, your organization and, yes, even the country where you work. If you are a professional employed as an accountant, lawyer or teacher you will want people to trust you so you should dress conservatively to gain this trust. On the other hand if you are an artist, athlete or carpenter doing creative or manual work you should dress more casually for action and comfort. Ideally your appearance must be based on a professional image, in sync with your job. Whether the appropriate dress is a uniform, business suit or a coverall, it must be worn with dignity and self confidence.

There are many sources available to help you in dressing wisely. There is much information on the internet and in books and magazines. But the easiest thing to do is simply take a look at what others in your profession are wearing and imitate them. You can also get advice from a relative or a friend who has more experience and style than you. In addition, speaking to your supervisor or a person in the Human Resource department in your company about it may also work in helping you to get your image right.

Crucial to your appearance is good personal hygiene which is a must in dressing for a professional image. It starts at the top of your head and ends at the soles of your feet. It includes your hair, hair-accessories, teeth, body odor, nails, body hair, make-up, jewelry and perfume fragrances.

When you dress for work, you are representing your company and your appearance should display this. How you dress sends a clear signal to the customer. If you want your customers to consider you as a professional, you have to look the part. In the following segment I have added some hints I learnt which helped me to maintain a good image and look professional.

The Professional Look

The following tips can be used as a personal guide to help portray oneself in the best possible manner both in and out of the office. This look provides a veneer that is neither gaudy nor ostentatious, but always complete. Much attention is placed on the *"little"* things. Extra space is provided alongside these tips for you to write down any changes you want to make that may help to improve your image.

PROFESSIONAL TIPS	PROFESSIONAL YOU
○ Hair ought to be clean and neatly styled away from the face. ○ Be wary of dandruff on your shoulders after brushing your hair, especially if your clothes are dark in color. ○ Extreme hairstyles are only for professionals whose job demands them. ○ Hair colors and wigs are now popular for both men and women but they should look as natural as possible to avoid being a distraction.	

PROFESSIONAL TIPS	PROFESSIONAL YOU
○ Adornments in hair should match your hair color and should not be obvious. Curlers should be used at home and never worn in public.	
○ Teeth should be clean and cavity free. Cavities are a source for bad breath so have regular dental checks especially if you are dealing face to face with customers. ○ Silver/gold teeth are no longer considered fashionable or a status symbol and it is recommended that they be replaced by porcelain fillings.	
○ All underclothing and hosiery should be changed before each work period.	

PROFESSIONAL TIPS	PROFESSIONAL YOU
○ Underwear should neither be provocative or obvious. ○ Lines caused by too tight underwear in both sexes are unsightly and distasteful.	
○ Bathe and use deodorant to avoid offensive body odors. ○ Change your brand of deodorant frequently and avoid scented ones. ○ Any person allergic to chemical deodorants can now access natural ones. ○ Fragrances should also be applied sparingly.	
○ Keep body hair to a minimum as hair traps odors. ○ Men with beards should keep them neatly trimmed beards.	

PROFESSIONAL TIPS	PROFESSIONAL YOU
○ Ladies should shave their legs and never wear stockings with unshaven legs.	
○ Hands/nails should be manicured and well presented. Nail polish if worn should be a quiet color.	
○ Most females look better with a little make-up to achieve that finished look. ○ Foundation or powder helps to give an even skin tone and keeps the shine of oily skin under control. ○ Make-up should not be obvious, it is used to enhance, and too much or too little could have equally negative effects.	

PROFESSIONAL TIPS	PROFESSIONAL YOU
○ Jewelry including earrings should be conservative and kept to a minimum with office attire. ○ Rings should be clean and free from soap film. ○ Watchbands should be conservative and in good shape. You want customers to notice and remember your competence and ability, not your Jewelry.	
○ Clothing is required to be appropriate for the occupation. For example mechanics wear coveralls not three piece suits. ○ Clothing should be clean and pressed at the start of the day.	

PROFESSIONAL TIPS	PROFESSIONAL YOU
○ It should be uncluttered and not draw attention to itself – except as a uniform or a professional outfit. ○ It should also be well fitting, not too loose or sloppy or baggy.	
○ When dressing use no more than two patterns in one ensemble. For example, patterned shirt and patterned tie should use a solid jacket. ○ Three solids however are allowed in one ensemble. ○ Choose patterns that compliment each other. Remember that patterns stand out and can easily become too busy.	

PROFESSIONAL TIPS	PROFESSIONAL YOU
○ Skirts should not be too short as sitting down then becomes a problem. ○ No glitter, rustle, transparent, body hugging or stretch fabric should be used in the workplace.	
○ Shirts should be pastel in color or as per uniform. ○ Sleeves should have one seam. ○ The collar should not be too tight. You should be able to comfortably pass your finger around the inside of the collar when it is buttoned. ○ The cuff should also stop where the wrists begins.	
○ Trousers for both men and women should be seamed- one seam only. Seams add structure and shape the leg.	

PROFESSIONAL TIPS	PROFESSIONAL YOU
○ Seams at the back of the trousers should start just under the buttocks and not from the waist. ○ As for trousers with pleats, the main centre pleat on each leg should be aligned with the seam at the front. ○ The pant leg should be hemmed so that the socks do not show while walking. Pants should be darker than the shirt.	
○ Ties for men should co-ordinate in color with simple patterns unless uniform design demands otherwise. ○ The tie is the focal point of the ensemble so care should be taken in your choice.	

PROFESSIONAL TIPS	PROFESSIONAL YOU
○ Thin ties create the illusion of "skinny" and fat ones create the illusion of "fat". Choose your tie based on your body structure. ○ The knot should be square and the tie should not be seen at the back of the collar. ○ The main rule is that the tie should touch the top of the belt even if you have a paunch. For those of you with a shorter torso the tie may be a bit longer, but should never pass the bottom of the belt. ○ Remember too that tie pins leave an irreparable hole in silk so a tie clip is recommended.	
○ Belts should match the shoes in color, design and texture (type of material used).	

PROFESSIONAL TIPS	PROFESSIONAL YOU
○ The exception to the rule is when the belt is made of the same fabric as the trouser/skirt/dress. Then the shoe color is optional. ○ The belt divides the body in half and draws attention to the area as it encircles the body. Be careful with the choice of size, color and design, especially if you are challenged in this area.	
○ Socks or stockings ought to not be obvious. ○ Stockings add a finish to the ensemble which is necessary for a professional look. They should be as sheer as possible since thick ones give the illusion of wooden legs. Flesh colored stockings are always the preferred choice.	

PROFESSIONAL TIPS	PROFESSIONAL YOU
○ Socks should be the same color as the pant hemline or darker than the pants. ○ White sports socks must never be worn at the office, unless you are a professional athlete.	
○ Shoes should be unadorned, clean and not have scuff marks. ○ Have shoe heels repaired. ○ For ladies pumps or court shoes are the only ones appropriate for the office. They may be closed or slingback and the toes must never show. ○ For the men, flat leather or leather soled slip-ons or oxfords are the appropriate footwear for the office.	
○ The physical appearance of fitness and health is an asset.	

PROFESSIONAL TIPS	PROFESSIONAL YOU
○ Extremes of over- or under- weight can have a negative effect as it is likely to promote an appearance of chronic ill health. ○ It is important that you adopt as healthy a lifestyle as possible with proper diet and exercise.	

Chapter 10
Appropriate Behavior at Work

"The greatest ability in business is to get along with others and influence their actions." (John Hancock)

In research done by reputable companies like Harvard University and Stanford Research Institute, the researchers concluded that one's success in business relied 85% on people skills and 15% on knowledge and technical skills. Based on this data it doesn't matter then how much knowledge and technical skills you have, your inability to relate to people will most likely cause you to fail.

How you relate to people and conduct yourself at work, your *"people skills"*, will have a negative or a positive impact on all your customers. Your behavior towards your colleagues, customers, bosses and subordinates as opposed to how you behave towards family and friends also require the use of different rules. Despite the differences, intrinsic to your behavior, whether you are dealing with your peers, supervisors, managers, the CEO or the customer, your modus operandi should always manifest respect, civility and a positive attitude.

Appropriate behavior for the office and good manners are the nuts and bolts needed to secure this concept of the adoption of customer service as a principle. These skills are essential since they also involve the building of respectful and warm relationships. Learning the acceptable behavior for the office is a must if you want to embrace success with both your internal and external customers.

Circle your answers to the questions below.

Question: Are you aware of how you behave at work?

YES / NO

Question: Do you know how others perceive your behavior?

YES / NO

Question: Is your appearance in sync with what your job is?

YES / NO

You should learn all you can about how to dress and behave at the workplace *"before"* you go to work. Your appearance and demeanor have a distinctive say in the aura you convey to others. If you dress well, have good posture and know your Ps' and Qs' you will exude confidence and it will positively impact on your relations with others. If you were to write a short paragraph describing your appearance and behavior, what would you compose?

Create a work of art which is YOU!

_____
_____
_____
_____
_____
_____

Give someone close to you to read what you wrote and ask his/her opinion of the person it describes. **Do you feel confident that he would say it was you?**

Chapter 11

Business Manners

"Manners – the final and perfect flower of noble character." (William Winter)

*I*n business manners, it is of the essence to be polite, gracious, sensitive, and tactful. Having basic good manners is a promising start to developing relationships and succeeding in your career. If you don't know the proper forms of address for colleagues, senior management, customers, government officials, religious officials, military titles etc. and you know that you have to interact with all of them then you must make it your business to learn what these are. There is also a correct way to greet and make introductions to customers, new co-workers and even friends and family at the workplace which you should also be familiar with. When to stand and when to sit during work interactions and how you answer and use the telephone have their own set of rules. Even your conversations at work matter and there are some topics you do not discuss.

The way you conduct yourself at work has a fundamental impact on your performance and can either hinder or help with your development in the company. Your behavior affects all your interactions with both your internal and external customers. As such, it is imperative to learn all you can about business manners and put them into practice as needed. There are books, on-line sites and other sources with pertinent information to help you learn all about business etiquette. They give the correct or acceptable ways to behave at work. Their information is based on a wide range of topics like interviews, table etiquette, meetings and other relevant skills.

Companies now also offer training courses to the public, to teach people these skills and help them learn how to effectively operate and behave at work.

With regard to business manners for customer service, the following are some pointers I learnt to enhance my dealings with customers. I have included space next to these for you to measure yourself against them. Jot down any changes you want to make to yourself which may help to improve you.

Business Manners for Customer Service

PROFESSIONAL TIPS	PROFESSIONAL YOU
○ When you are greeting customers you rise and go to meet them.	
○ You must use their name once you know it, within your next three sentences.	
○ If you are acknowledging your colleagues (internal customers) remember to always be polite and respectful.	
○ Use their name, smile and ensure you make eye contact.	

PROFESSIONAL TIPS	PROFESSIONAL YOU
○ When you address your bosses use the same method and remember the onus is on you to be the first to greet them. ○ Even if you are sometimes ignored, don't take it personally, continue to extend polite greetings.	
○ The general rule for making introductions is to introduce the person being presented last. ○ In a social setting, the person being introduced first depends on gender and age. However in a business setting the person to be introduced first is the more important one with the higher rank or authority. ○ If however you are introducing a customer	

PROFESSIONAL TIPS	PROFESSIONAL YOU
or a government official he outranks even the CEO. **You must introduce the customer first.** ○ It is also important if you are seated to always stand if you are being introduced, despite your gender. If it is difficult to stand because of circumstances, at least bend forward or rise slightly. ○ It is also recommended that you learn the correct pronunciation of peoples' names and titles.	
○ Shaking hands is an acceptable way to greet others in the Western world. However if you are in a foreign country it is advisable that you learn the acceptable ways to greet others.	

PROFESSIONAL TIPS	PROFESSIONAL YOU
○ A hand shake should be firm, last for 3 seconds and have at least 2 – 3 pumps. ○ Please do not continue shaking a person's hand throughout the introduction.	
○ Hugs, kisses and any form of touching do not belong in a business environment ○ In a business/social function it is acceptable to kiss your spouse, however it should be a simple peck on the cheek.	
○ Never keep customers waiting for more than 2 -3 minutes. If a longer time lag is unavoidable, an alternative is to tell them how long the delay will be and offer to reschedule.	

PROFESSIONAL TIPS	PROFESSIONAL YOU
○ Always be polite, courteous and sensitive to their needs. ○ Keep in mind if they do not get what they want, the interaction should always be a positive one, which will ensure that they continue to do business with you. Also do not keep your colleagues or other staff members waiting unnecessarily since this will result in strained and ruffled relationships ○ Remember you should always be courteous to your staff, treat them fairly and be friendly and approachable.	
○ To demonstrate respect towards older people you always stand to meet them.	

PROFESSIONAL TIPS	PROFESSIONAL YOU
○ If the elderly person is a customer you not only stand you also do all you can to help in every way possible.	
○ In business the distinction is status so remember to stand to greet some one who is of a higher status than you.	
○ If you have to supervise people who are older than you this requires sensitivity on your part without compromising company's standards.	
○ Keep your personal life private and do not discuss your own problems at the office.	
○ An office romance is a definite thumbs down and is considered to be totally unprofessional.	

PROFESSIONAL TIPS	PROFESSIONAL YOU
○ If you have to work with your spouse or with someone with whom you share a personal relationship remember to be professional and leave the romance for after working hours. ○ On the other hand, dealing with sexual harassment at the office must be handled promptly and directly. Remember if you are made to feel uncomfortable and your work is being affected you may be sexually harassed. If the offender continues despite your request for him/her to stop, then please take it to the appropriate and relevant authority in the company for assistance.	

PROFESSIONAL TIPS	PROFESSIONAL YOU
○ At work gender discrimination should be avoided. Also do not discriminate because of a person's size, height or race.	
○ Confidential company business, anything negative about the company or its management, political views, sex and off-color jokes and even religious views should not be discussed at work.	
○ In addition you must also choose the language you use to communicate with others. For example swear words and obscene language do not belong in a work environment, neither does chauvinistic terms like, "sweetheart" or even "love."	

PROFESSIONAL TIPS	PROFESSIONAL YOU
○ You also want to avoid using racist expressions, slangs and jargon. ○ Remember to keep your voice level low and avoid using foreign accents to try to be someone you are not. ○ Refrain from gossiping and be discreet in your dealings with others.	
○ Meetings are unavoidable and the key is to show up on time - if not early. ○ Ask where to sit if you are not assigned a seat. ○ Ensure that you arrive prepared, having done your home work. ○ Follow the agenda. ○ Be wary of slouching as this body language will send a message of a lack of interest.	

PROFESSIONAL TIPS	PROFESSIONAL YOU
○ With regard to telephone etiquette, remember to answer it promptly, within three rings if possible. ○ Always identify who you are and what your position is. ○ If you are a receptionist then after a greeting, identify the name of your company. ○ Be sure to confirm that it is convenient to continue the call, then simply explain the purpose of your call. ○ Use the person's name as soon as you can. ○ Remember to listen and also to make listening noises so that the other person knows you are still there. Repeat directions, numbers, dates and times to ensure you have the correct information.	

PROFESSIONAL TIPS	PROFESSIONAL YOU
○ It is a good idea to also smile as you talk since it helps to make your voice sound more friendly and confident.	
○ Mobile phones should be turned off during interviews. ○ During training sessions, meetings and most work activities they should be put on a vibrate mode. ○ Most companies have rules with regard to mobiles and you should observe these. ○ Regarding cell phone etiquette, the main rule which applies to customer service is that front line staff are normally required to turn off cell phones at all times during work.	
○ E-mail etiquette is also important and the main rules are:	

PROFESSIONAL TIPS	PROFESSIONAL YOU
○ Do not write the entire message in capital letters, as this is equivalent to shouting. ○ Reread what you are sending before you send it. ○ Do not "Reply to all" unless you know who the "all" are. ○ Don't e-mail unless you have to, most people are already bogged down with too much work. ○ All other general communication rules also apply to e-mails.	
○ After work, remember too that customers will still identify you by the company you work for even if you are off-duty and away from office premises. Conduct yourself therefore in a manner that endorses an unquestionable impression.	

80　*Chapter 11: Business Manners*

There are many more tips I can add to these, however the important thing to remember is that *"Good manners will open doors that a good education cannot"* (Clarence Thomas). There is absolutely no excuse for you to be impolite and ungracious to your customers. *"Treat everyone with politeness even those who are rude to you – not because they are nice but because you are."* (Unknown) If you've adopted customer service as a principle, I believe that you will do all you can to ensure that your customer interactions proudly display your knowledge of good business manners.

Appropriate dress and grooming requirements and good business manners are compulsory to enable one to practice good customer service skills. They lay the foundation on which you can comfortably foster lasting relationships and advance a flourishing career. They are the prerequisites needed to triumphantly embrace other principles like respect, courtesy, sensitivity and many more. With confidence in your ability to dress and act in a manner that encourages healthy habits and displays characteristics of a knowledgeable and approachable individual, you cannot falter. I can whole heartedly assure you that if you are dressed appropriately and feel confident and self assured you will also act accordingly. This ground work is vital for you to have a positive effect on your dealings with all of your customers. It builds rapport and encourages goodwill, which results in satisfied customers and also gives you a delightful sense of pride and achievement – another clear-cut *"win/win"* situation.

"Prepare yourself for the world, as the athletes used to do for their exercises; oil your mind and your manners, to give them the necessary suppleness and flexibility, strength alone will not do" (4th Earl of Chesterfield, Phillip Dormer Stanhope). Anyone can learn how to make the necessary changes to improve his image. The key is – he must want to.

Chapter 12
Delivering Quality Customer Care at the Workplace in a Nutshell

"The first step binds one to the second."
(French proverb)

*L*earning about what is, and how to, demonstrate excellent customer service is easy. Putting it into practice takes more effort and requires a conscious commitment and dedicated perseverance. On board the aircraft we not only referred to our customers as our guests, we treated them as we would our guests. To do this it was mandatory to board the aircraft one hour before they did, to check;

- *emergency equipment*
- *catering*
- *stores*
- *pillows*
- *blankets and other requirements.*

Customers were welcomed warmly at the door, ushered to their seats and made to feel at home and comfortable as quickly as possible, If you were expecting company, would you not for starters;

- *Be nicely dressed*
- *Have prepared a delicious meal*
- *Made sure the guest room had clean sheets and*
- *Checked that there were clean towels in the bathroom?*

In the same way you have to begin preparations to deliver good service to your customers. This preparation in a nutshell is a three step process.

- *The first step is learning all you can about business manners, your job, the organization, and the products and service you are offering, (with or without formal training) from the company. This knowledge will increase your confidence and make you feel more at ease, as you greet your customers.*
- *Next you begin by dressing for the role, in what is the conventional and correct dress.*

- *You are now ready to greet your customers. Make eye contact, smile and use the customer's name as soon as you can. The greeting after all sets the pace for the interaction and it is the key to its success. <u>Remember you only have one opportunity to create a good first impression.</u>*

On board the aircraft, my guests' names were printed on their boarding passes and when checking for their assigned seats on it, I would also verify their names and say *"Welcome aboard Mr. & Mrs. Williams, my name is Joy and we are very happy to have you here with us today."* Many passengers did not realize this and were amazed that I knew their name. Almost always I could see the pleasure in their faces when I called them by their names, since it made them feel special and welcomed. It usually opened the door for the start of a very cordial relationship. You can also always introduce yourself to your customer even if you are wearing a name tag to start building rapport.

- *Using the customer's name is very important.*
- *It makes the customer feel like a person instead of a number.*
- *It shows respect*

- *It establishes the fact that he has your undivided attention.*
- *A key technique in building rapport is the use of a person's name.*

Having now completed the three steps process and properly greeted your customer, you can now move on to determining his needs, then meeting and surpassing them. To do this you need to use excellent communication and listening skills.

Chapter 13

Communication

"Communication is depositing a part of yourself in another person."
(Anonymous)

What is communication? What do writing in a journal; watching television; talking on the phone and reading a book commonly share? They are all means of communication. The word communicate may also be used to identify activities that do not involve people. For example, animals communicate with one another as do electronic devices. When we talk about communication however, we usually refer to activities involving people, like you and I and the customer. How would you describe communication?

Communication is:

_____
_____
_____
_____
_____
_____
_____
_____
_____
_____
_____
_____
_____
_____
_____
_____
_____
_____
_____

Communication has also been defined as:

- *"The means through which people exchange feelings and ideas with each other."*
- *"The transfer/exchange of information and the understanding of that information, from one person to another."*

These meanings may seem simple enough but much more needs to be said since many of us have difficulty communicating with each other. Embracing success through customer service involves the use of effective communication skills.

Think about it, before any dialogue even takes place, communication has already begun. When a customer walks into your place of work, your senses immediately assimilate information about that person. Your senses of sight, smell, touch... immediately go into over-drive and your brain draws on past experiences for answers. For example, you think of something your parents may have told you or what you may have read in books. Depending on what the brain reports, you form a perception of the customer and may begin to feel comfortable or ill at ease. The same thing is also happening to the customer and assumptions are made on both sides, which can lead to miscommunication.

I recall dealing with a passenger on a New York flight travelling to Guyana whose behavior was a bit strange. She was uncommunicative and distant and despite my attempts to be friendly and welcoming, she was unresponsive. I decided to just keep on being polite and gracious, regardless of her attitude. I only disturbed her if it was necessary and generally extended all the courtesies to her that I would normally do to my passengers. The flight had an intransit stop in Trinidad and this involved a crew change on the ground in Trinidad. It was while waiting to hand over the flight there, she approached me and quietly thanked me for giving her *"the space she needed."* She then explained that she was travelling to Guyana to join her family for a funeral. Their mother had passed on unexpectedly and she was still trying to come to terms with it. I extended my condolences to her and felt really relieved that I had not assumed she was just an obnoxious person.

It can be so easy to jump to the wrong conclusions, based on how we *"see"* things. However when you adopt customer service as a principle, (*"A moral rule or set of ideas which guides behavior"*) it allows you to focus on others and not on yourself. By simply continuing to do your job as best as you possibly can, despite distractions, you sometimes score, big time. I was so grateful that I was of some help to her at a time she really needed it. It also reinforced a very important lesson, to never *"judge a book by its cover"*.

The following communication model is simple and straightforward to better understand the communication process.

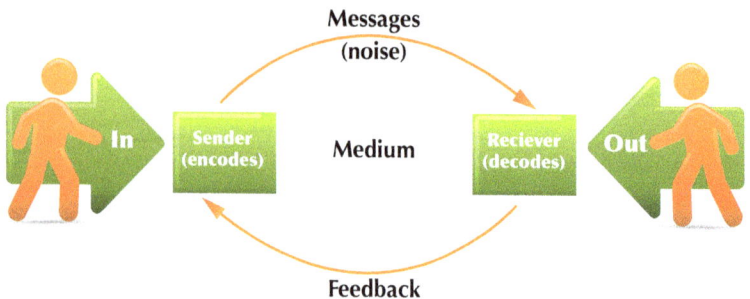

For communication to be effective it must be two-way and it involves much more than words. It also involves tone and body language. Research shows that in terms of communication:

- *"Words account for 7%*
- *Intonation for 38% and*
- *Body language accounts for 55%."*

In a telephone conversation:

- *"Words will account for 18% and*
- *Intonation will account for 82%."*

Using the above communication model, let us travel from one component to the other to examine the communication process closely.

Sender to Receiver

Between the sender and receiver is where you will find the message which has to be interpreted. During this journey there are many distractions that may affect its understanding. Therefore the message must be clear and the best medium must be chosen to convey it. For example, if you send an email or fax and do not get confirmation of a response, have you communicated? No, you have simply sent a message, because for communication to be effective a message has to do more than just be sent.

Even if you choose the right words and the best medium there are also other factors that can affect the message.

- *Distractions*
- *noises*
- *accents*
- *education*
- *prejudices*
- *speed over clarity*
- *health*
- *interpretation*
- *lack of knowledge*
- *status*
- *body language and emotions*

These can cause distortion and confusion to the

message. It can also get quite confusing if your words or verbal expression are saying something and your body language or your non-verbal action contradicts it.

One of the factors which really affected my communications on board the aircraft, was that of foreign languages. We operated flights to Caracas, Germany and Switzerland, and because I could only speak English well, communicating with people who spoke other languages became quite a challenge for me. It always made me, thankfully, realize that as human beings we could use other forms of communication, like sign language, to assist us in crossing these barriers. Face to face communication, after all, gives us the greatest opportunity to communicate clearly and effectively. This is where we can successfully use our non-verbal actions to assist us.

Receiver to Sender

Between receiver to sender is feedback, and listening must take place. Listening plays a major role in the communication process. Listening is much more complicated and involved than the physical process of hearing. When we hear, we merely observe someone else's thinking. When we listen, we think along with the speaker. Hearing is passive and listening is active. It is said that we listen at four levels;

- *Level 1 is making sense of sound and distinguishing words. It is more like an "awareness." Example: Driving with the radio on and listening to music.*

- *Level 2 is when understanding begins. Concentration on what is being said and differences in words and their meanings become significant. Example: You recognize the song and may even sing along.*

- *Level 3 is when you distinguish fact from fantasy – analysis is required on the part of the receiver. Example: You actually form your own opinion of the words of the song and may even disagree with what the singer is singing.*

- *Level 4 is the highest level and requires the greatest amount of skill and concentration. It involves the added dimension of empathy, enabling the receiver to understand what is being said from the sender's point of view. Example: If it is a romantic song of lost love and you may have experienced this, or because the song is a sad one you are able to feel and experience the singer's pain.*

Being able to listen and understand requires practice and effort. We can also listen with our eyes for the nonverbal messages. To improve our listening skills and practice active listening we must first want to do so. In Steven Covey's book, *"The 7 Habits of Highly Effective People"* he writes about developing a habit to *"Seek first to understand and then to be understood."* We can only do this by listening. To improve our listening skills we can:

- *Recap, repeat or go over what the customer requested, to let him know that you understand what he needs. In other words you are confirming that what he needs is what he actually requested.*

- *Ask open-ended questions as opposed to close-ended ones. These require more than a YES/NO answer and need to be explained. Explanations help to clarify what is being said. It also encourages the customer to:*

> *- Share more information*
>
> *- Speak more freely and*

- Let you know what is important to him.

- **Empathize with the customer and tell him that you understand how he feels. Put yourself in his shoes and let him know that you would feel exactly like him if it were you.**

Listening is essential to effective communication. To listen does not necessarily mean to always agree. It does mean that when you disagree you do so agreeably.

ALSO is an acronym we can use to practice our listening skills.

A- Avoid distractions – visual, auditory or mental

L- Look – maintain eye contact

S- Summarize – this demonstrates understanding

O- Open mind – Do not prejudge

Listening is the foundation for all effective communication. What people say is important to them, even if it may not at times be important to you. We can all learn to listen better to be more effective in our dealings with our customers. How well do you listen? To determine if you are a good listener, answer each of the following questions honestly and objectively based on what you do, not on what you would like to do or believe you ought to do. Place a check next to the answer of your choice after every question.

ARE YOU A GOOD LISTENER?

When taking part in a conversation do you:

1. Make eye contact and face the speaker to make sure you can hear?

( ) Yes ( ) Sometimes ( ) No

2. Avoid distractions, listen actively and wait until the speaker finishes talking before you respond?

( ) Yes ( ) Sometimes ( ) No

3. Never assume what someone is going to say simply by how he looks?

( ) Yes ( ) Sometimes ( ) No

4. Recognize your own prejudices and try to keep an open mind?

( ) Yes ( ) Sometimes ( ) No

5. Listen also with your eyes to body language as well as your ears to words?

( ) Yes ( ) Sometimes ( ) No

6. Summarize and repeat to demonstrate understanding and confirm what was said?

( ) Yes ( ) Sometimes ( ) No

7. Empathize with the speaker to better understand what is being said?

( ) Yes ( ) Sometimes ( ) No

If your answers are "Yes" you know that you are a good listener. However if they are not, try to identify and improve in the areas that you feel you need to.

After listening you can then give feedback to the Sender to show that there is understanding. This can only occur if;

- *the message was clear*
- *active listening took place.*

Communication is the place where both the sender and the receiver have the same interpretation and understanding of the message. Of course, if there is a need for further clarification, this is where it will also take place. Then the process will be repeated.

We have now come full circle, from sender to receiver and back from receiver to sender and so effectively communicated. To improve our relationships at work and to satisfy both our internal and external customers we have to sharpen our communication skills. Anyone can develop and improve their skills in this area if they choose to do so.

A friend shared with me his thoughts about communicating with his customers. He likened his conversations to interviews and believed that while he was interviewing his clients, he also believed that his clients were at the same time interviewing him. At the end of the *"interview"* they would both decide if their relationship would work for their mutual benefit. It was therefore very important to him that he behaved in a respectful, helpful and empathic manner to communicate trust and commitment. He believed that relating discussions to interviews kept him on track and focused and so was better able to determine and meet his customers' needs.

When you consider the preparation that should take place before you attend an interview, you can easily understand why this works. One would have:

- *Dressed properly.*
- *Have copies of relevant documents.*
- *Learnt all you could have about the potential job and the company.*
- *Graciously greeted the interviewer(s) with a firm handshake.*
- *Made eye contact with a polite greeting and*
- *Generally observed the right protocol that goes with the territory.*

This surely is very similar to what I have been saying all along. It reeks of preparation and preliminary ground work.

It is a good idea for you to discover what works for you personally to keep you on track. US President Harry S. Truman kept a sign on his desk with the phrase *"The buck stops here"* This was to remind him to not shirk his responsibilities and stay on course. I am sure that in whatever you choose to help keep you focused you will find the guiding principles mentioned enshrined in your choice.

We want to succeed in our chosen careers and it is very important to use effective communication skills to realize this. I read a Chinese proverb which said, *"If you want one year of prosperity, grow grain. If you want ten years of prosperity, grow trees. If you want a hundred years of prosperity grow PEOPLE."* Another name for people is **CUSTOMERS.**

Chapter 14

Skills for Challenging Customers

"No life is so hard that you can't make it easier by the way you take it."
(Ellen Glasgow)

Chapter 14: Skills for Challenging Customers   103

Challenging customers bring wonderful opportunities to put the knowledge of many of your new skills to the test. These customers are the impatient, angry, or confused ones, with unrealistic expectations.

These expectations may be from bad experiences or from personal problems. The key to handling them is to focus on what their needs are and not their moods. It is important not to take their behavior personally. Even so, dealing with them can be quite challenging since automatically you want to react to them in the same manner they are addressing you. Steven Covey in his book, *"The Seven Habits of Highly Effective People"* writes that as human beings we have *"choice"* and it is this choice which differentiates us from animals. You can then choose how to always react and in dealing with challenging customers you have to be very careful of the choices you make. The answer lies in not trying to change their behavior but in focusing on managing the interaction to meet their specific need at that time. Your ability to actively listen to them will help to diffuse their charged emotions. Skills that will help you are:

- *Pay attention by actively listening.*

- *Confirm and ensure that you know and understand what the problem is.*

- *Explain step by step what you can do or the reason why you can't do it.*

- *Offer alternative solutions to solve the problem if possible.*

- *"Counting to ten" as a silent moment has proven to help calm one and, at the same time, it will give you some time to focus on your next step.*

- *Agree and empathize with the customer's criticisms as this will help to soothe things. Expressions like, "I understand how you must feel." or "That must have been really upsetting" can help calm troubled waters.*

- *Apologize even if it's not your fault. You can be sorry for the customer's perceived ordeal. It is really okay to express sympathy for what he says he has experienced. It can actually start calming him right away so that you can get on with resolving the issue. When you apologize to a customer you are not accepting blame or trying to end an altercation, you may just be expressing your understanding and empathy.*

- *Ask for assistance from a supervisor or colleague if you need it. Sometimes referring the problem to someone who is in a better position to help will prevent a further escalation of the problem. Accept your limitations and be prepared to accept help from your colleague.*

These skills in practice demonstrate professional behavior. They help you focus on the concept that service is a principle (*"A truth or belief that is accepted as a base for reasoning and action"*) and guide your behavior to meet any challenging situation. It ensures that the interaction ends on a positive note.

The acronym *SERVICE* gives us a snapshot of how to consistently deliver excellent customer care using the concept that service is a principle.

S   *– Satisfy the customers and remember the process starts even before the greeting.*

E   *– Exceed the customers' expectation, which is easy when you apply the concept, that service is a principle, making it possible to efficiently handle any situation.*

R   *– Respect your customers by being polite and considerate.*

V   *– Value and appreciate your customers and at the same time, give them value for their money.*

I   *– Interest and involvement in the customer service interface, make the process successful.*

C   *– Communicate effectively with your customers, by using their names and actively listening to them.*

E   *– Embrace success by demonstrating knowledge and skills for guaranteed satisfaction through all your customer service interactions.*

Chapter 15

Benefits

"Look not a gift horse in the mouth,"
(Proverb)

When you apply the concept that good customer service is a principle, *("A truth or belief that is accepted as a base for reasoning and action.")* it will produce many benefits. The dictionary defines a benefit as *"Something that promotes or enhances well-being"* or as *"an advantage"*. A good way to recognize a benefit in good customer service is when you see customers returning again and again to buy your products and services. Here are some other benefits from positive customer service encounters:

- *Helps to preserve jobs, yours and others.*
- *You have fewer hassles and more satisfied customers.*
- *You have less stress when you focus on solving problems.*
- *You will learn and practice skills for professional growth.*

- *It will increase your self-confidence.*
- *You get recognition from customers and staff.*
- *More importantly it will create goodwill for the organization*
- *You keep customers for life and so improve sales and profit.*
- *You have so much more fun.*

We are all customers and we should treat others in the way we expect to be treated ourselves. The choice is a personal one to improve your customer service skills so that you can contribute to producing all these benefits. By choosing your behavior in dealing with others to ensure a positive outcome, you are putting into practice the concept that good service is a principle. The result is – boundless benefits and well-contented customers.

Conclusion

"The ultimate test for us of what a truth means is the conduct it dictates or inspires." (William James)

I am sure that by now you understand how important it is to adopt customer service as a principle. If you want to instinctively and involuntarily react to customers in a manner which supports excellent care, respect and goodwill you really do not have any other choice. You now know:

- *What it means to adopt customer service as a principle*
- *How to identify your customers*
- *What customers generally expect*
- *What good service really means*
- *The impact this service can have on the profitability of a company*
- *The importance of learning how to dress and behave at work*
- *How to improve your communication and listening skills*
- *How to better handle challenging customers*
- *How to recognize the benefits of great service which results in lasting relationships and repeat business*

Quality service care is a rare and beautiful experience, and can bring immeasurable satisfaction to both the customer and yourself. You need to periodically contemplate how you behave to ensure that you are consistently delivering superior customer service. There are many times when you get caught up in the rush of deadlines and other time-constraint issues and you lose your focus; you are merely human after all. Thankfully you have principles to guide you and bring you back on course. I believe that adopting customer service as a principle (*"A truth or belief that is accepted as a base for reasoning and action."*) is the key to unlocking all these beliefs which guide your behavior.

You are an individual customer who interacts with other customers on an on-going basis. You want to treat them in exactly the same way that you would like to be treated. If you adopt customer service as a principle I have absolutely no doubt that you will be anchored to a solid foundation which will ensure that you excel with your customers. Having a positive attitude will naturally be your way of life.

A positive attitude supports the optimistic *"half-full"* answer to *"Is this glass half-full or half-empty?"* This allows you to focus on going the extra mile when delivering good customer service. It means that you have the opportunity to actually now *"walk your talk"*. Walking your talk usually requires you do the little things that make such big differences. That extra touch that could simply be, *"Let me help you with that"* or *"Yes, I understand"* or *"It's no trouble at all"*.

I found this beautiful poem which describes exactly what I mean.

> *"Little stones make big mountains,*
> *Little steps can cover miles.*
> *Little acts of kindness*
> *Give the world its biggest smiles.*
>
> *Little words can soothe big troubles,*
> *Little hugs can dry big tears.*
> *Little candles light the darkness,*
> *Little memories last for years.*
>
> *Little dreams can lead to greatness*
> *Little victories to successes*
> *It's the little things in life*
> *That brings the greatest happiness."*
>
> (Unknown)

It is always useful to remember that a little kindness goes a long way. When you adopt customer service as a principle, it really becomes a habit to be thoughtful, helpful and kind.

Individually, we can each make a positive difference to the way we deliver service. Remember the oyster, (*"I cannot remove it, so I think I'll improve it"*) the next time you make a decision about how you behave as you continue to serve others. I truly believe that if you keep the concept of adopting service as a principle, (*"a set of ideas which guides"* your *"behavior"*) in the forefront of your mind, you will not only embrace success but when you look at the glass, your "cup will over flow."